HOUGHTON MIFFLIN HARCOURT

JOURNEYS

Program Authors

James F. Baumann · David J. Chard · Jamal Cooks
J. David Cooper · Russell Gersten · Marjorie Lipson
Lesley Mandel Morrow · John J. Pikulski · Héctor H. Rivera
Mabel Rivera · Shane Templeton · Sheila W. Valencia
Catherine Valentino · MaryEllen Vogt

Consulting Author
Irene Fountas

HOUGHTON MIFFLIN HARCOURT
School Publishers

Hello, Reader!

Do you know what it's like on the Moon? Have you ever wondered where maple syrup comes from? Can you guess what it is like to travel in a donkey cart? In this book, you will discover the answers to these questions and more.

Open your book and see what discoveries are inside!

Sincerely,

The Authors

Exploring Together

Big Idea We discover new things every day.

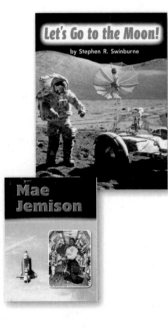

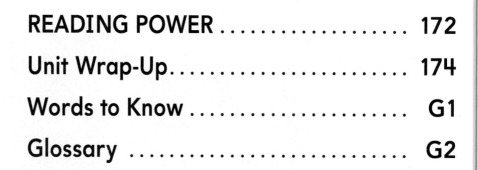

Exploring Together

Unit 4

Big 💡 Idea

We discover new
things every day.

Paired Selections

Read Together

✔ **WORDS TO KNOW**
HIGH-FREQUENCY WORDS

think

bring

before

light

because

carry

show

around

Vocabulary Reader

Context Cards

Words to Know

Read Together

- Read each Context Card.

- Choose two blue words. Use them in sentences.

1 **think**

What do you think space is like?

2 **bring**

Spaceships can bring astronauts to space.

10

3 before

Astronauts practice flying **before** their trip.

4 light

People feel very **light** floating in space.

5 because

Astronauts like to jump **because** it is fun!

6 carry

Astronauts **carry** tools to work with.

7 show

Pictures **show** us what the Moon is like.

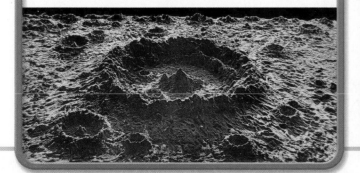

8 around

You can see clouds all **around** Earth.

Background

Read Together

✓ WORDS TO KNOW **Astronauts** Astronauts are people who travel around space. They feel light there. Before they go, they think about what to bring. Sometimes they carry special cameras because they want to show people at home what space is like.

Things in Space

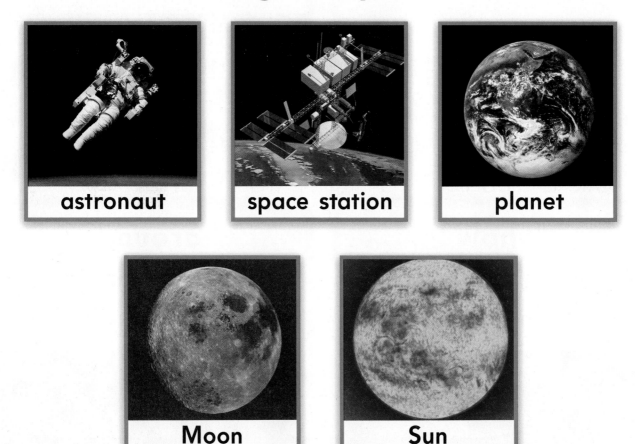

astronaut

space station

planet

Moon

Sun

12

Comprehension

✓ **TARGET SKILL**   Main Idea and Details

Good readers think about the topic when they read. They look for the **main idea**, or most important idea, about the topic. Then they think about the **details**, or facts, that tell more about the main idea.

As you read **Let's Go to the Moon!**, name the topic. Then look for details that tell more about the main idea. Use a web like this one to tell about the main idea.

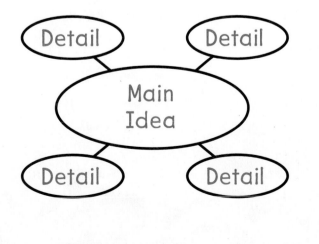

Let's Go to the Moon!
by Stephen R. Swinburne

✔ **WORDS TO KNOW**

think	because
bring	carry
before	show
light	around

✔ **TARGET SKILL**

Main Idea and Details
Tell important ideas and details about a topic.

✔ **TARGET STRATEGY**

Question Ask questions about what you are reading.

GENRE
Informational text gives facts about a topic.

Meet the Author

Stephen R. Swinburne

Steve Swinburne has never been to the Moon, but he loves to travel and explore new places here on Earth. His trips have brought him close to bears, bobcats, and wolves! He has written many books about the things he has seen.

Let's Go to the Moon!

written by Stephen R. Swinburne

Essential Question

What is important to know about the Moon?

15

Blast Off!

Would you like to fly to the Moon? Let's go!

10, 9, 8, 7, 6, 5, 4, 3, 2, 1 . . . BLAST OFF!

The Flight

It can take four days to get to the Moon.
A rocket helps us blast into space. We ride
in the space ship at the top of the rocket.

The surface of the Moon is dusty and has many craters.

There are no plants or animals on the Moon. There is no water or air. The Moon has rocks, dust, and craters. A crater is a big hole.

Space Suits

This is astronaut Ronald Evans wearing his space suit.

It's time to put on our space suits. Space suits help keep our skin safe from the very hot sun and the very cold shade.

The space suits have air in them so we can breathe. Now we are dressed for our walk on the Moon.

Moon Walk

Walking on the Moon is fun.
We can take big, light steps.

We are very light because the
Moon has less gravity than Earth.

We carry space tools with us.
We have jobs to do here.

Moon Rocks

We find rocks and bits of dust to bring back home. We will show the rocks to people back on Earth.

Lunar Rover

We drive around in our lunar rover. It's even more fun than walking in our fat space suits. Look at all the dust the lunar rover kicks up!

✔️ **STOP AND THINK**

Main Idea and Details
What did you learn about the lunar rover?

27

Taking Pictures

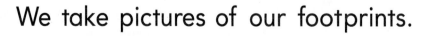
We take pictures of our footprints.

We take a picture of our space ship, too.

Our flag is up!

Let's take one last look before we go. We see rocks and dust.

Let's Go Home

It's time to go back home.

What is it like to be on the Moon?

It's strange and fun at the same time.

When you look up and see the
Moon, what do you think?
Our Moon is beautiful!

Your Turn

Ask the Author

Write Questions

Think about what you discovered in **Let's Go to the Moon!** What if you could meet the author of this selection? Write four questions you would like to ask him.

PERSONAL RESPONSE

Turn and Talk — Moon Jobs

Talk with a partner about the different jobs astronauts do on the Moon. Tell why you think each job is important.

MAIN IDEA AND DETAILS

35

Mae Jemison

Connect to Science

GENRE

A **biography** is a true story about events in a real person's life.

TEXT FOCUS

A **time line** shows the order of events. Use the time line on page 38 to retell in order the important events in Mae Jemison's life.

Mae Jemison

by Debbie O'Brien

Mae Jemison was born in Alabama. Mae knew she wanted to be a scientist when she grew up.

Mae studied very hard in college and became a doctor. She went to Africa because she wanted to help sick people there.

Here is Mae Jemison on the space shuttle. ▶

Later, Mae became an astronaut. She had to learn many things before she could go into space.

At last, Mae was ready to fly in the space shuttle. The astronauts had to bring equipment with them. They had to carry food, too. Mae could move around easily in space. She felt light as a feather.

Now Mae has her own company. She wants people to think about science. She tries to show people how science helps them every day.

Mae becomes a doctor.

Mae starts her company.

1980 1981   **1987**   **1993   1995**

Mae becomes an astronaut.

Making Connections

Read Together

Text to Self

Connect to Science What if you were an astronaut? Write about what you would do in space.

Text to Text

Tell Main Ideas Tell a partner the most important things you learned about being an astronaut. Speak clearly.

Text to World

Draw and Share Find a picture of a real planet. Pretend that you have gone there. Draw a picture of things you discovered. Tell about the planet.

Grammar

Read Together

Questions A sentence that asks something is called a **question**. A question always begins with a capital letter and ends with a question mark.

> **W**hat is it like on the Moon**?**
>
> **A**re there any mountains**?**
>
> **D**o plants and animals live there**?**

Write each question correctly. Use another sheet of paper.

1. what do astronauts do on the Moon

2. do they wear space suits

3. can they jump really far

4. does their buggy go fast

5. why do they take pictures

✏ Grammar in Writing

When you revise your writing, try using some questions.

Write to Narrate

✓ **Ideas** If you are writing **sentences** about yourself, be sure all your sentences are about one main idea.

Kim wrote about a cave she found. Later, she took out a sentence that didn't belong.

Revised Draft

My sister and I found a cave.

It was very dark inside.

~~I like the woods.~~

 **Writing Traits Checklist**

✓ **Ideas** Do all my sentences tell about one main idea?

✓ Does each sentence begin with a capital letter?

✓ Does each sentence end with the correct mark?

42

Look for the main idea in Kim's final copy.
Then revise your writing. Use the Checklist.

A Big Surprise

My sister and I found a cave.

It was very dark inside.

We had a big surprise when some bats flew out!

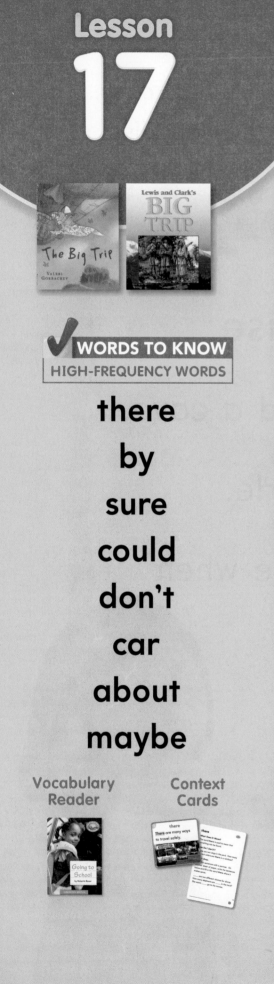

WORDS TO KNOW
HIGH-FREQUENCY WORDS

there
by
sure
could
don't
car
about
maybe

Vocabulary Reader

Context Cards

Words to Know

- Read each Context Card.

- Make up a new sentence that uses a blue word.

1

there

There are many ways to travel safely.

2

by

Wear a helmet when traveling by bike.

3 sure

Be sure to buckle your seat belt!

4 could

You could walk to the bus with a buddy.

5 don't

Don't stand while the school bus is moving.

6 car

A car should always stop at a STOP sign.

7 about

These children know about bike safety.

8 maybe

Maybe you can help someone be safe.

Background

✔ WORDS TO KNOW **Taking a Trip**

There are many ways to travel. You can go by bus, car, or train. Maybe you will go by plane. When you go, be sure to bring a book or a toy. It could be a long trip, and you don't want to be bored! Name some more ways to travel. Tell about them.

Ways to Travel

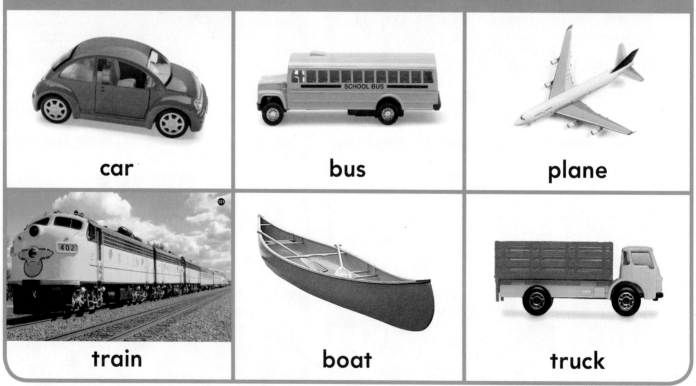

car

bus

plane

train

boat

truck

"I am going to take a trip far away,"
Pig said to Goat one day.
"How will you go?" asked Goat.

The Big Trip

by
VALERI GORBACHEV

Essential Question

How are ways to travel the same and different?

"Let me think for a moment," said Pig. "Maybe I will go by bike—that will be a very nice trip."

"Oh, dear," said Goat. "You could fall off a bike."

"Ah," said Pig. "Then I will drive a car."

52

"It's not a good idea, Pig," said Goat.
"A car can break down!"

"Oh," said Pig. "Then I will
go by horse on my trip."

54

"I'm not sure about that," said Goat.
"Horses can be very jumpy!"

"Okay," said Pig. "Then I am going to go by donkey cart—a donkey is very quiet."

"Not good, not good," said Goat.
"Donkeys can be very stubborn!"

✔ **STOP AND THINK**

Compare and Contrast
How do Pig and Goat each feel about taking a trip by donkey cart?

"Then I will go by train," said Pig.

"Oh, Pig, oh, Pig," said Goat,
"a train could get stuck in a tunnel!"

"Good point, Goat," said Pig.
"Then I will fly by plane."

"What if the engine stops!" said Goat.
"You'd have to parachute."

"True," said Pig. "Then I will go by
hot air balloon."

"The hot air balloon could have a hole!" said Goat.

"Okay. I will not travel by land. I will not travel by air. I will go by sea," said Pig. "On a ship."

"Oh, no!" exclaimed Goat. "Don't do it! The ship could run into a reef when passing through fog."

"Or run into a heavy storm at sea, and there are sharks all around at sea, so many, you couldn't count them!"

"And you could find yourself alone on a desert island in the middle of the ocean with pirates that could come on that desert island by pirate ship!"

"Stop!

Stop! STOP!"

exclaimed Pig.

65

"I could fall off a bike
break down in a car
get thrown by a horse
never get there with a donkey
or get stuck on a train.
I might have to parachute from a plane
or from a hot air balloon
and traveling by ship could bring
me many troubles!"

"So, I will not go anywhere," said Pig.
"Having a big trip is a very scary thing."

"Unless . . . ," said Goat, looking at Pig,

"you go with a friend."

Say each sentence with a partner. Decide if it is a statement or a question. Then write the sentence correctly on a sheet of paper.

1. our family is taking a trip

2. where are you going

3. how will you get there

4. we will fly on a plane

5. may I come, too

Grammar in Writing

When you revise your writing, use some different kinds of sentences to make your writing interesting.

Write to Narrate

☑ **Ideas** When you write **sentences** about yourself, help readers picture what you did. Use details that tell where and when.

Sam wrote about a trip he took. Later, he added words that tell where he was.

Revised Draft

My family went camping.

by a lake

We set up our new tent.
^

 Writing Traits Checklist

☑ **Ideas** Do my sentences have details that tell where and when?

☑ Did I write clear letters and use a space between words?

☑ Does each sentence end with the correct mark?

76

Look for words that tell where and when in Sam's final copy. Then revise your own writing. Use the Checklist.

Final Copy

Our Camping Trip

My family went camping.

First, we set up our new tent by a lake.

The next day I was so happy because we rode in a canoe!

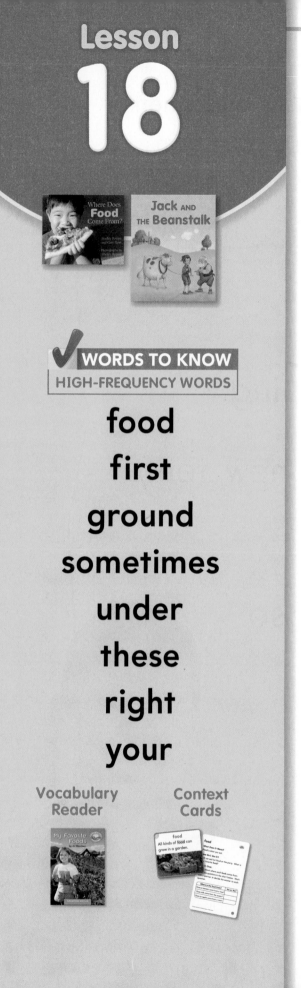

✓ **WORDS TO KNOW**
HIGH-FREQUENCY WORDS

food
first
ground
sometimes
under
these
right
your

Vocabulary
Reader

Context
Cards

Words to Know

● Read each Context Card.

● Ask a question that uses one of the blue words.

1
food
All kinds of food can grow in a garden.

2
first
The seeds are planted in the soil first.

3 ground

Keep the **ground** near the plants wet.

4 sometimes

Sometimes pumpkins grow very big!

5 under

Carrots grow **under** the ground.

6 these

These tomatoes are ready to be picked.

7 right

You can pick pea pods **right** off of the vine.

8 your

What will you plant in **your** garden?

Background

✔ WORDS TO KNOW **From Farm to Table**

Do you know where your food comes from?
Many fruits and vegetables grow on farms.
First, farmers plant seeds. Some plants,
like carrots, grow under the ground.
Others, like beans, grow above the ground.
Farmers pick these vegetables at the right
time. Sometimes they send them to stores
for us to buy.

Comprehension

Read Together

✔ TARGET SKILL   Author's Purpose

Authors write for many reasons. They
write to share a message or to make you
laugh. They write to tell
facts and details to help
you learn something.

wheat

As you read **Where Does Food
Come From?**, think about why the
authors wrote the story.

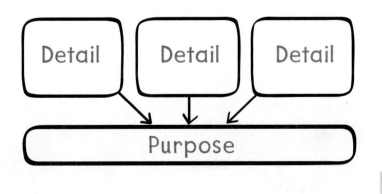

| Detail | Detail | Detail |

Purpose

JOURNEYS DIGITAL   Powered by DESTINATIONReading
Comprehension Activities: Lesson 18

81

✓ **WORDS TO KNOW**

food	under
first	these
ground	right
sometimes	your

✓ **TARGET SKILL**

Author's Purpose Tell why an author writes a book.

✓ **TARGET STRATEGY**

Summarize Stop to tell important ideas as you read.

GENRE
Informational text gives facts about a topic.

Shelley Rotner

Shelley Rotner started writing books about things that interested her daughter. If you have questions about the world around you, the answers might well be in a book by Ms. Rotner!

Meet the Author

Gary Goss

Gary Goss says, "I love food and creating. I also love working with kids." Mr. Goss has written a children's cookbook called **Blue Moon Soup**.

Where Does **Food** Come From?

written by
Shelley Rotner
and
Gary Goss

Photographs by
Shelley Rotner

Essential Question

Why do authors write nonfiction?

Cocoa beans are seeds.
They grow on cocoa trees.
Chocolate is made by crushing
and cooking cocoa beans.
Hot cocoa is made from chocolate.

Apples are fruits that grow on trees.
An apple is picked right off the tree.
Apple juice is made by pressing the
juice from apples.

Potatoes are vegetables.
These vegetables grow under the ground.
French fries are made from potatoes.

Wheat is a grain that grows in fields.
Flour can be made by crushing the wheat.
Bread is made from flour.

Rice is a grain.

It grows in wet fields called paddies.

Rice that you eat is made by cooking the grain.

Corn is grain that grows in fields.
Popcorn is made from corn.
First you heat it, and then it pops.

Milk comes from cows—
or sometimes from goats.
Butter, cheese, and ice
cream are made from milk.

The eggs you eat are laid by hens.
The hens live on farms.
There are many ways to cook eggs.

Tomatoes grow on vines. Ketchup is made from tomatoes.

✔ STOP AND THINK

Author's Purpose Why do the authors show a picture of ketchup near tomatoes?

Honey is made by bees.

They bring the nectar of flowers to the hive.

Maple syrup is made from sap.
The sap drips from maple trees.

Where does your favorite food come from?

🔍 Match Game

Find a Match Work with a partner. Draw four foods on four cards. Then draw where the foods come from on other cards. Lay all the cards face down. Take turns flipping over two cards. Keep them if they match.

PARTNERS

Turn and Talk — Food Facts

What do the authors of this selection want you to learn? Talk about it with a partner. Then take turns telling facts you learned. AUTHOR'S PURPOSE

Jack AND THE Beanstalk

Connect to Traditional Tales

✓ WORDS TO KNOW

food	under
first	these
ground	right
sometimes	your

GENRE

A **fairy tale** is an old story with characters that can do amazing things.

TEXT FOCUS

Many fairy tales end with **storytelling phrases**, such as **happily ever after**. Find these words. Why do you think the storyteller uses them?

Jack AND THE Beanstalk

Once upon a time, there was a boy named Jack. He and his mom had no money for food because someone had taken their goose. Sometimes, it would lay golden eggs for them!

Jack went to sell their cow. He met a man. "I will trade these special beans for your cow," the man said.

Jack came home. His mother was mad.
She threw the beans on the ground.

Soon a tall beanstalk grew. Jack climbed
it. At the top was a huge castle. Inside, Jack
found his goose in a cage under a table!

Then Jack heard, "FEE! FIE! FOE! FUM!
Look out! Here I come!"

It was a giant! First Jack grabbed the
goose. Then he ran right out the door.

Jack climbed down the beanstalk as fast as he could. He chopped it down.

Now Jack and his mother were safe, and they had their goose. They all lived happily ever after.

Making Connections

Read Together

Text to Self

Write a List Make a list of foods you like to eat. Tell classmates about them.

Text to Text

Tell About Food Jack's beanstalk started out as tiny beans. Tell about beans and other vegetables you have eaten.

Text to World

Connect to Technology Use the Internet to find out how people grow your favorite food. Draw a picture that shows what you learned.

Grammar

Read Together

Names of Months, Days, and Holidays The names of **months** in a year, **days** of the week, and **holidays** begin with a capital letter. When you write a date, use a **comma** between the day of the month and the year.

Names of Months

We planted seeds on **M**ay 14, 2011.

Days of Week

My dad cooked soup on **F**riday.

Holidays

My family eats turkey on **T**hanksgiving.

Write each sentence correctly. Use another sheet of paper. Tell a partner what you did to correct each sentence.

1. Ali began school on september 8 2010.

2. She has science club every friday.

3. There was no school on memorial day.

4. Last wednesday our class took a field trip.

5. School ended on june 14 2011.

Grammar in Writing

When you proofread your writing, be sure you have written the names of months, days, and holidays correctly.

Write to Narrate

Read Together

✓ **Sentence Fluency** A good **friendly letter** is not boring! Use different kinds of sentences to make your writing lively and interesting.

Ned drafted a letter about a special meal he had. Then he added a question.

Revised Draft

Then we tasted all the food.
Can you guess my favorite?
∧ The apple pie was best of all.

Writing Traits Checklist

✓ **Sentence Fluency** Did I write different kinds of sentences?

✓ Does my letter have all five parts?

✓ Did I use capital letters and commas correctly?

Look for different kinds of sentences in Ned's final copy. Then revise your writing. Use the Checklist.

Final Copy

March 8, 2010

Dear Mario,

My school had a potluck supper. First, each class cooked something. Then we tasted all the food. Can you guess my favorite? The apple pie was best of all.

Your friend,
Ned

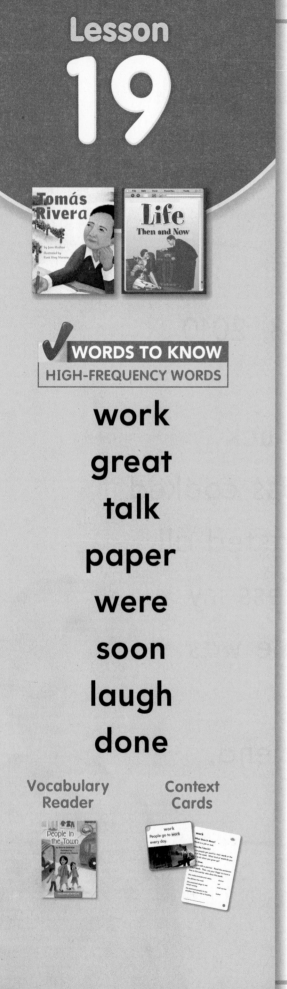

✔ **WORDS TO KNOW**

HIGH-FREQUENCY WORDS

work

great

talk

paper

were

soon

laugh

done

Vocabulary Reader

Context Cards

Words to Know

Read Together

- **Read each** Context Card.

- **Use a blue word to tell a story about a picture.**

1

work

People go to work every day.

2

great

She did a great job baking this cake!

3 talk

He likes to **talk** with customers at his job.

4 paper

This artist does his work on **paper**.

5 were

The farmers **were** very busy today.

6 soon

Soon it will be time to go to lunch.

7 laugh

A silly clown makes everyone **laugh**.

8 done

He goes home when the work is **done**.

113

Background

WORDS TO KNOW **Writing a Book** Most books begin with an idea. Sometimes a writer talks about the idea with a friend. If the idea is funny, the writer hopes the friend laughs! Soon it is time to start writing. A writer may write on paper. It is a lot of work. It feels great when the book is done. What kind of book would you write if you were a writer?

Things a Writer Uses

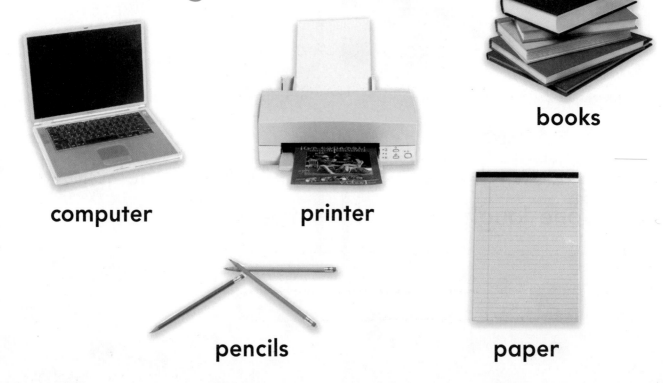

computer

printer

books

pencils

paper

Comprehension

✓ **TARGET SKILL** Conclusions

Good readers use details to figure out things about a story that an author may not tell them. This is called drawing **conclusions**. Readers use details from the text, pictures, and what they know from their own life to draw conclusions.

> What is your conclusion?
> What clues helped you?

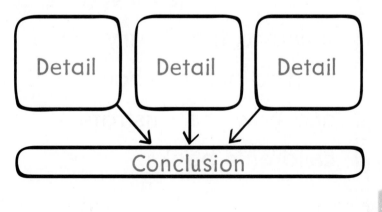

As you read **Tomás Rivera**, use story clues and what you already know to draw conclusions.

```
┌─────────┐   ┌─────────┐   ┌─────────┐
│ Detail  │   │ Detail  │   │ Detail  │
└────┬────┘   └────┬────┘   └────┬────┘
     └──────────┐  │  ┌──────────┘
        ┌───────▼──▼──▼───────────┐
        │       Conclusion        │
        └─────────────────────────┘
```

Main Selection

✓ **WORDS TO KNOW**

work	were
great	soon
talk	laugh
paper	done

✓ **TARGET SKILL**

Conclusions Use details to figure out more about the text.

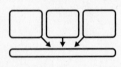

✓ **TARGET STRATEGY**

Monitor/Clarify Find ways to figure out what doesn't make sense.

GENRE

A **biography** tells about a real person's life.

Meet the Author

Jane Medina

Jane Medina is both a teacher and a writer, just like Tomás Rivera. She began writing when she was a teenager. Since then, she has written books of poems in Spanish and English.

Meet the Illustrator

René King Moreno

As a young girl, René King Moreno loved to draw and paint. She also loved going to the library. She studied art in school, and now she illustrates children's books.

Tomás Rivera

by Jane Medina

illustrated by
René King Moreno

Essential Question

What clues help you figure out how characters feel?

117

Tomás Rivera was born in Texas.
Tomás and his family went from
place to place picking crops.

Tomás helped pick crops all day. It was
a lot of work. When the work was
done, Tomás would talk with his Grandpa.

"Come quick!" Grandpa called.
"It's time for stories!"

"You tell the best stories!"
Tomás said. "I wish I could
tell great stories, too."

The next day, Grandpa said, "We can get lots of stories for you, Tomás." "When?" asked Tomás.

"Quick, hop in!" Grandpa said with a wink.
"I will show you!"
Grandpa drove the truck up the road.

"This is a library," said Grandpa.
"Look at all the books!" gasped Tomás.

"Read all you can, Tomás. It will help you think of lots of stories," said Grandpa.

✔ STOP AND THINK
Conclusions
Why does Grandpa bring Tomás to the library?

There were lots of books for Tomás to read.
Some were funny and made him laugh. He
read about boats, trains, and cars. He
dreamed of space. Soon Tomás was thinking
of his own stories.

Tomás began telling his stories.
Then he wrote them on paper.

When he was a grown-up, Tomás got a
job as a teacher. He still wrote stories.

Tomás Rivera's stories tell about people picking crops, just as his family did. Lots of people read his books.

Now his name is on a big library.
Many people go to the library.
They get books, just as Tomás did.

A Favorite Book

Write Sentences Tomás likes to read many different kinds of books. What kinds of books do you like to read? Write about one of your favorite books. Tell what it is about and why you like it.

PERSONAL RESPONSE

Turn and Talk — Library Visit

Look at pages 124–126 with a partner. How do you think Tomás feels about the library? Talk about the clues that helped you decide.

CONCLUSIONS

Connect to Social Studies

GENRE

Informational text gives facts about a topic. This online encyclopedia entry was written to give true information.

TEXT FOCUS

A **chart** is a drawing that lists information in a clear way.

File   Edit   View   Favorites

Life
Then and Now

The way people live changes over time. Today families live differently than in the past.

In the past, many jobs were done by hand. Now people have great machines for doing work.

In the past, people wrote letters on paper and sent them by mail. Now people can send messages right away. They talk on cell phones or send e-mails by computer.

In the past, families listened to radio programs. Now families laugh as they watch TV programs.

Family Life

We use many of the same things that people used in the past.

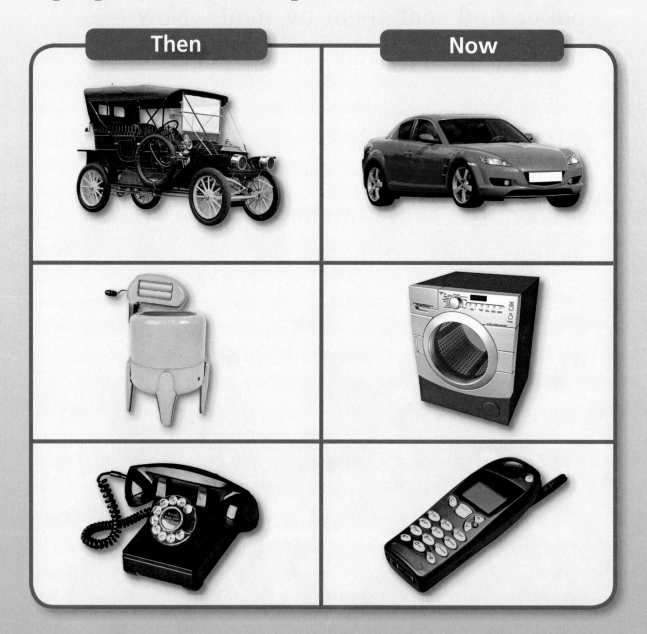

Then	Now

Think about the future. Soon families may do things in a whole new way!

Making Connections

Text to Self

Connect to Social Studies Tell about a job you would like to have. Speak clearly so listeners can understand you.

Text to Text

Recognize Purposes Were **Tomás Rivera** and **Life Then and Now** written to give information or to make you laugh? What did you learn?

Text to World

Create an Invention Draw an invention that could help children in the future with their schoolwork. Tell ways it could change how children work.

Grammar

Read Together

Verbs and Time Verbs can tell what is happening now, in the past, or in the future. Verbs with **will** or **going to** tell about the future.

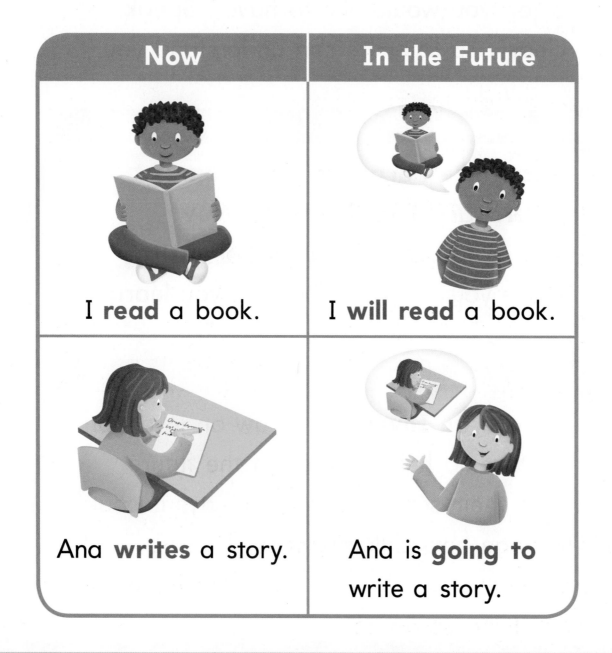

Now	In the Future
I **read** a book.	I **will read** a book.
Ana **writes** a story.	Ana is **going to** write a story.

136

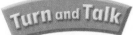

Read each sentence with a partner. Find the sentences that tell about the future. Then rewrite the other sentences to tell about the future. Use another sheet of paper.

1. I will go to the library.

2. I am going to find books.

3. I buy some books at the store.

4. My dad is going to read them to me.

5. I write a poem.

Grammar in Writing

When you revise your writing, be sure that sentences that tell about the future use **will** or **going to**.

Write to Narrate

Read Together

☑ **Organization** Before you write a **personal narrative**, you need to plan what to say.

Ava told her story to Zoe. That helped Ava choose events and details for her story.

Exploring a Topic

 Prewriting Checklist

 Did I choose an interesting topic?

☑ Are the events on my chart in order?

☑ Do my details tell who, what, where, and when?

Look at the details Ava put in her chart.
Plan your own story using a Flow Chart.
Write sentences or notes in order to tell
about events.

Planning Chart

First

bus to city

Next

saw dinosaur

Last

apples in park

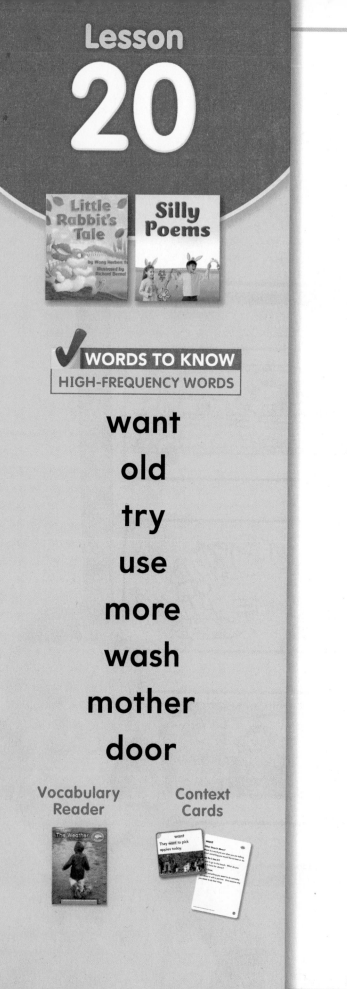

Little Rabbit's Tale

Silly Poems

✓ **WORDS TO KNOW**
HIGH-FREQUENCY WORDS

want

old

try

use

more

wash

mother

door

Vocabulary Reader

Context Cards

Words to Know

● Read each Context Card.

● Use a blue word to tell about something you did.

1

want

They want to pick apples today.

2

old

This little apple tree is not very old.

3 try

They try to find the best apples.

4 use

Use a ladder to reach the high apples.

5 more

No more apples will fit in here!

6 wash

Be sure to wash the apples.

7 mother

Ben's mother helps us make a pie.

8 door

Open the oven door when the pie is done.

door

Background

✔ **WORDS TO KNOW** **A Silly Mistake** One thing can cause more things to happen. You want to read a book. So you sit by a tree. Then you feel something on your head. You think it is a bug! You run and yell. You shake your hair. Then you use a hose. You try and wash it out. Your mother comes out the door. She says, "It's just an old leaf!"

Apple Tree

leaves

apple

branches

trunk

Comprehension

✓ **TARGET SKILL** Cause and Effect

When you think about **cause and effect**, you think about how one story event leads to another. The cause is the reason something happens. The effect is what happens.

Cause An apple falls on Little Rabbit's head.

Effect Little Rabbit wakes up.

As you read **Little Rabbit's Tale**, keep track of what happens and why it happens.

What happens?	Why?

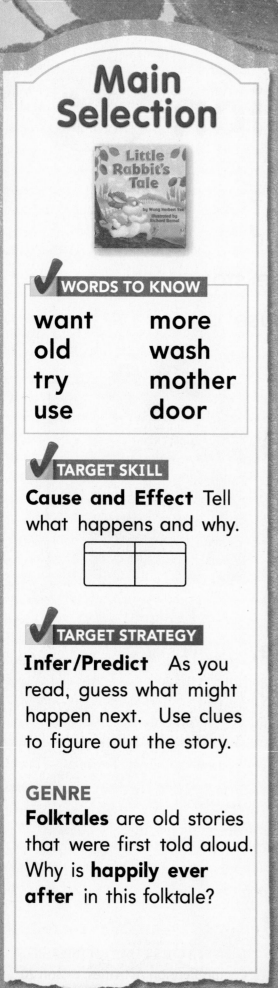
Meet the Author

Wong Herbert Yee

Wong Herbert Yee loves to write and draw. "Little Rabbit reminds me of my daughter Ellen," he says. "Her favorite animal is a rabbit. I try to put a rabbit in every story I write!"

Meet the Illustrator

Richard Bernal

Richard Bernal started drawing when he was in the first grade. He says, "I like to have fun when I make pictures. See if you can find the letters R.B. marked on a tree!"

Little Rabbit's Tale

by Wong Herbert Yee
illustrated by Richard Bernal

Essential Question

What makes a story funny?

Little Rabbit sleeps under an old apple
tree. Just then, the wind starts to blow.
The branches shift in the wind.

Thump!

Something hits Little Rabbit.

"Oh, no! The sky is falling!" yells
Little Rabbit. "I've got to try to
tell everyone!"
Little Rabbit hops off to find Goose.

Goose sits in his rowboat.
The tip of his rod starts to twitch.
"There's no time to fish!" yells
Little Rabbit. "The sky is falling!"

"Let's go, Little Rabbit! We need to go
tell Beaver!"
Goose and Little Rabbit use the rowboat.
They go up the stream.

Goose peeks inside.

Beaver is eating a snack.

"There's no time to eat," says Goose.

"Let's go! The sky is falling!"

"Oh my!" says Beaver. "We need
to go tell Turtle."
Beaver, Goose, and Little Rabbit
dash up the hill.

✔ STOP AND THINK
Cause and Effect
What happens when Goose tells
Beaver that the sky is falling?
Find the words that tell.

Turtle sleeps under a log.
TAP, TAP! Beaver taps on Turtle's
shell. Turtle peeks out.
"There's no time to sleep," says Beaver.
"Let's go! The sky is falling!"

"Oh, no!" yells Turtle. "What can we do?"
"Let's run back home," says Little Rabbit.
"I want to tell my mother!"

Turtle, Beaver, Goose, and Little Rabbit
run fast. They hop over the log,
dash down the hill, . . .

and jump into Goose's rowboat.
Then they go as fast as they can
down the stream.

Little Rabbit hops in the door.
"Mother, the sky is falling!"
"Who told you such a thing?"
asks Mother Rabbit.

"Beaver told me!" says Turtle.

"Goose told me!" says Beaver.

"Little Rabbit told me!" says Goose.

"Well let's just go outside and look
at the sky," says Mother Rabbit.

Just then, the wind starts to blow.
The branches shift in the wind.

Something hits Little Rabbit.

"Oh, no! The sky is falling!" yells
Little Rabbit.

"The sky is not falling," laughs
Mother Rabbit. "An apple just fell
from the apple tree!"

"I didn't get to catch a fish," says Goose.
"I didn't get to eat my snack," says Beaver.
"I didn't get to sleep," says Turtle.

"I've got a plan," says Little Rabbit.
"Can my friends eat with us?"
"Yes," says Mother Rabbit. "Go wash
your hands while I get more plates."

Hooray!

Little Rabbit has a nice meal with his friends. After that, they all have homemade apple treats!

The friends lived happily ever after!

Your Turn

The Sky Is Falling!

Act It Out Act out **Little Rabbit's Tale** with a group. Decide who will play each character. Show how the characters feel as you act out the story.

SMALL GROUP

Turn and Talk — Funny Finish

Look at page 158 with a partner. How is it different from the first time the apple hits Little Rabbit? Talk about what makes **Little Rabbit's Tale** a funny story.

CAUSE AND EFFECT

Connect to Poetry

want	more
old	wash
try	mother
use	door

GENRE

Poetry uses the sound of words to show pictures and feelings. Listen for rhyme and rhythm as you read.

TEXT FOCUS

In **choral reading,** two or more people read aloud together.

Readers' Theater

Silly Poems

READER 1   Here is an old joke. What kind of stories do rabbits want to hear?

READER 2   I know! They like stories with hoppy endings!

BOTH   Let's try reading this funny bunny poem together.

Funny Bunny

Here's a bunny
With a nose so funny.
His home is a hole in the ground.

When a noise he hears,
He perks up his ears,
And then jumps into the ground.

READER 1 Here is a poem by Langston Hughes.

READER 2 Who is more afraid, the elephant or the mouse? I'll read the first four lines. You read the rest.

Elephant,

Elephant,

Big as a

House!

They tell me

That you

Are afraid of a

Mouse.

Write a Silly Poem

Use rhyming words and the words mother, wash, and door in your poem. Use words that tell what things look like or sound like.

Making Connections

Little Rabbit's Tale
by Wong Herbert Yee
Illustrated by Richard Bernal

Silly Poems

Text to Self

Silly Sentences Write sentences to tell classmates about something silly that you saw or did.

Text to Text

Use Describing Words Think of the rabbit in the selections. Take turns with a partner. Tell what a rabbit looks like.

Text to World

Connect to Social Studies Find out where apples grow. Use the symbols on a map. Tell what you find out, using words like **north**, **south**, **east**, or **west**.

Grammar

Read Together

Prepositions A preposition is a word that joins with other words to help explain where something is or when it happens. A **prepositional phrase** is a group of words that starts with a preposition.

The rabbit napped **under** a tree.
It was **before** the apple fell.

Read each sentence with a partner. Find the preposition or prepositional phrase in each sentence. Write them on another sheet of paper. Talk with your partner to decide whether the preposition tells about where or when something happened.

1. Ted read a book before dinner.

2. He was in an apple tree.

3. There was a sound above his head.

4. A bird flew around him.

5. He was right by its nest!

Grammar in Writing

When you revise your writing, be sure to include prepositional phrases to tell about where and when.

Write to Narrate

Read Together

✓ **Word Choice** In a good **personal narrative**, exact details help readers picture what happened.

Ava wrote about a special day. Later, she changed words to make them more exact.

Revised Draft

Then we went to a museum.
rocks, stars, and dinosaurs
I saw ~~stuff~~.
                ^

Revising Checklist

✓ Do my sentences have exact details?

✓ Did I use order words?

✓ Did I spell words correctly?

Look for details in Ava's final copy. Then revise your own writing. Use the Checklist.

Final Copy

A Great Day

Last Friday, my mom and I had an adventure. First, we took a bus to the city. Then we went to a museum. I saw rocks, stars, and dinosaurs. Last, we gladly ate some apples in the park.

Read the next two selections. Use details to draw conclusions about each selection.

A Very Cold Place

Some people like the North Pole. It takes a long time to get there. You can get near the North Pole by boat or by plane, but you still have to walk to get there.

People get around by sled. The sleds are pulled by special dogs. Their fur is very thick.

If you go to the North Pole, you will see a lot of snow. You might also see polar bears on the way. Seals live there, too. You might even see a whale or two!

Ice Fish

The South Pole is a very cold place. It is colder than the North Pole! The ocean near the South Pole is like a big bowl of ice and water. The water is so cold, bits of ice float on it.

More than ninety kinds of fish live in this water. One kind is the ice fish. Ice fish live in cold, cold water. Blood would freeze in this water. Ice fish have something special in their blood that keeps it from freezing. This lets them live in the cold, icy water.

Unit 4 Wrap-Up

The Big Idea

Let's Explore! Real places can have surprises. Write a story about a surprise you have found in a place near home.

Listening and Speaking

Apple Surprise Read about apples in **Where Does Food Come From?** Tell your class how you think people make apple juice from apples. What happens first, next, and last?

174

Words to Know

Unit 4   High-Frequency Words

16 Let's Go to the Moon!

think	because
bring	carry
before	show
light	around

17 The Big Trip

there	don't
by	car
sure	about
could	maybe

18 Where Does Food Come From?

food	under
first	these
ground	right
sometimes	your

19 Tomás Rivera

work	were
great	soon
talk	laugh
paper	done

20 Little Rabbit's Tale

want	more
old	wash
try	mother
use	door

Glossary

A

apple
An **apple** is a fruit with red, yellow, or green skin. Jose´ picked a red **apple** from that tree.

B

beaver
A **beaver** is an animal that has large front teeth and a flat tail. We saw a **beaver** swimming in the water.

born
Born means brought to life. The kittens were **born** yesterday.

C

chocolate
Chocolate is a kind of food that is dark and sweet.
Chocolate is my favorite kind of candy.

crater
A **crater** is a large hole in the ground. We saw a picture
of a big **crater** on the Moon.

D

desert
A **desert** is a large dry area of land.
The **desert** has a lot of sand.

E

engine
An **engine** is a kind of machine that
burns oil, gas, or wood. My sister's
car has an **engine** that makes it go very fast.

exclaimed

To **exclaim** means to say something in a strong way.
"Watch out!" Dillon **exclaimed**.

F

family

A **family** is a group of people who often live together.
Our **family** lives in the city.

favorite

Favorite means what you like the most. My **favorite**
pet is a dog.

footprints

A **footprint** is the mark
a person or an animal
leaves. We looked back
and saw our **footprints** in
the sand.

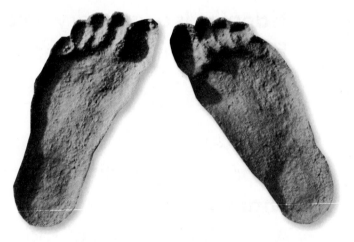

G

goose

A **goose** is a kind of bird that has a long neck. The **goose** is sitting on her nest.

gravity

Gravity is the force that pulls us to the ground. **Gravity** is stronger on Earth than it is on the Moon.

H

happily ever after

Happily ever after is a storytelling phrase that means happy from that time on. The three little pigs lived **happily ever after**.

hooray

Hooray is a word that people shout when they are happy. When Jim won the race, we all yelled **hooray**!

I

island

An **island** is an area of land that has water all around it. Risa and her family took a boat to the **island**.

J

jumpy

Jumpy means moving in a way that isn't smooth. Tino moved in a **jumpy** way that made him spill his milk.

L

library

A **library** is a place where books are kept. I borrow a book from the **library** each Monday.

lunar

Lunar means having to do with the Moon. My grandpa remembers watching the first **lunar** landing on TV.

O

oh

Oh is a word that shows strong feelings. "**Oh** no!" said Mom when the car did not start.

P

paddies
A **paddy** is a field of rice. The people worked hard in the rice **paddies**.

parachute
When you **parachute**, you use something that opens up and helps you float to the ground. After he jumps from the plane, Elliott will **parachute** to the ground.

people
People means more than one person. Lots of **people** came to hear Ben sing.

R

rabbit
A **rabbit** is an animal with long ears and soft fur. My pet **rabbit** likes to hop.

rocket
A **rocket** is something that flies in space. A hundred years ago, no one believed we would send a **rocket** to the Moon.

rover

A **rover** is something that moves from one place to another. The **rover** moved across the Moon's surface.

S

says

Says means tells. Mom **says** that Dad will be home soon.

sky

The **sky** is the air above the ground. I saw a plane fly high in the **sky**.

stories

A **story** is writing that tells what happens to people or to other characters. My grandma tells **stories** about what she did when she was a girl.

stubborn

If you are **stubborn**, that means you don't change your mind easily. My little sister can be **stubborn** when she wants her way.

T

teacher

A **teacher** is a person who teaches others. My mother is a math **teacher**.

Texas

Texas is a state in the United States of America. We like to visit our grandpa in **Texas**.

told

Told means said something to someone. My friend **told** me a funny joke today.

Tomás Rivera

Tomás Rivera was a writer and a teacher. **Tomás Rivera** began writing when he was a young boy.

travel

To **travel** means to go and visit another place. Next summer we are going to **travel** to South America.

troubles

Trouble is something that makes it hard to know what to do. That place has had many **troubles** over the years.

tunnel

A **tunnel** goes under ground or water to help people get from one place to another. They drove through a **tunnel** to get to the city.

V

vegetables

A **vegetable** is a plant or a part of a plant that you can eat. You should eat **vegetables** because they are good for you.

Acknowledgments

The Big Trip written and illustrated by Valeri Gorbachev. Copyright © 2004 by Valeri Gorbachev. Reprinted by permission of Philomel Books, a Division of Penguin Young Readers Group, a member of Penguin Group (USA) Inc. All rights reserved.

"Elephant, Elephant" from *The Sweet and Sour Animal Book* by Langston Hughes. Copyright © 1994 by Ramona Bass and Arnold Rampersad, Administrators of the Estate of Langston Hughes. Reprinted by permission of Oxford University Press and Harold Ober Associates, Inc.

"Funny Bunny" originally published as "Here's Bunny" from *Ring A Ring O'Roses: Finger Plays for Pre-School Children.* Published by Flint Public Library. Reprinted by permission of Flint Public Library.

Where Does Food Come From? by Shelley Rotner and Gary Goss, photographs by Shelley Rotner. Text copyright © 2006 by Shelley Rotner and Gary Goss. Photographs copyright © 2006 by Shelley Rotner. Reprinted by permission of Millbrook Press, a division of Lerner Publishing Group. All rights reserved.

Credits

Photo Credits

Placement Key: (t) top; (b) bottom; (l) left; (r) right; (c) center; (bkgd) background; (frgd) foreground; (i) inset.

8a (c)Ariel Skelley/Age FotoStock America, Inc.; **8b** spread (c)John Warden/Stone/Getty Images; **8b** inset (c) 1996 C Squared Studios; **10** (t) (c) JUPITERIMAGES/ BananaStock/Alamy; **10** (b) (c)NASA/Handout/Getty Images News/Getty Images North America/Getty Images; **11** (tl) (c) MAXIM MARMUR/Staff/AFP/Getty Images; **11** (tr) (c)Corbis; **11** (cl) (c)NASA/CORBIS; **11** (cr) (c)NASA - Apollo/digital version by Science Faction/Getty Images; **11** (bl) (c)Sean Sexton Collection/CORBIS; **11** (br) (c)NASA/Corbis; **12** (tl) Corbis; **12** (tc) Stock Trek; **12** (tr) NASA; **12** (bl) Digital Vision/Getty Images; **12** (br) Corbis; **13** (c)Stocktrek/Corbis; **14** (c)Courtesy of Steve Swinburne; **14-15** (c)NASA-Apollo/Science Faction/Getty Images; **16-17** (c)Ctein/Getty Images; **18** (c)NASA-Apollo/Science Faction/ Getty Images; **19** (c)NASA/Science Source/ Photo Researchers; **20** (c)NASA/Stringer/Time & Life Pictures/Getty Images; **21** (c)NASA/ Photo Researchers, Inc.; **22-23** (c)Keystone/ Stringer/Getty Images; **24** (c)NASA; **25** (c) MPI/ Stringer/Hulton Archive/Getty Images; **26-27** (c) NASA; **28** (c)NASA; **29** (c)NASA; **30** (c)NASA; **31** (c)CORBIS; **32-33** (c)Brand X/SuperStock; **34-35** (c)Robert Karpa/Masterfile; **35** (inset) (c) NASA-Apollo/Science Faction/Getty Images; **46, 47** HMCo; **62** (l) (c)Independence National Historical Park; **62** (r) (c)Independence National Historical Park; **62-63** (bkgd) (c)Purestock/Getty Images; **63** (inset) (c)Montana Historical Society; **64-65** (c)Purestock/Getty Images; **65** (inset) (c) D. Hurst/Alamy; **70** (c)Shelley Rotner; **71** (inset) (c)Shelley Rotner; **71** (bkgd) Shelley Rotner; **72** (l) (c)Shelley Rotner; **72** (cr) Shelley Rotner; **73** (c)Shelley Rotner; **74** (bkgd) (c)Shelley Rotner;

74 (inset) Shelley Rotner; **75** (c)Shelley Rotner; **76** (c)Shelley Rotner; **77** (c)Shelley Rotner; **78** (l) (c)Shelley Rotner; **78** (tr) Shelley Rotner; **79** (c)Shelley Rotner; **80** (c)Shelley Rotner; **81** (c) Shelley Rotner; **82** (r) (c)Shelley Rotner; **82** (l) (c) Shelley Rotner; **83** (l) (c)Shelley Rotner; **83** (r) (c) Shelley Rotner; **84** (l) (c)Shelley Rotner; **84** (r) (c) Shelley Rotner; **85** (bl) (c)Shelley Rotner; **85** (r) (c)Shelley Rotner; **86** (tl) (c)Shelley Rotner; **86** (br) Shelley Rotner; **86** (bl) Shelley Rotner; **86** (tr) Shelley Rotner; **87** (bkgd) Shelley Rotner; **87** (br) (c)Shelley Rotner; **88-89** (c)foodfolio/Alamy; **89** (c)Thomas Northcut/Getty Images; **90** (c)C Squared Studios/Getty Images; **90** (c)C Squared Studios/Getty Images; **90** (c)C Squared Studios/ Getty Images; **90** (c)C Squared Studios/Getty Images; **90** (c)C Squared Studios/Getty Images; **90** (c)C Squared Studios/Getty Images; **90** (butter) (c)Artville; **91** (c)Brand X Pictures; **93** (c)Randy Miller/CORBIS; **98** HMCo.; **152** (c)Gabe Palmer/ Alamy; **152** (t) (c)1996 C Squared Studios; **154** (c) PhotoDisc/Getty Images; **155** (c) S. Alden/ PhotoLink; **156** (c) PhotoDisc/Getty Images; **156** (c) PhotoDisc/Getty Images; **157** (c) Brand X Pictures; **159** (c) Image Ideas, Inc.; **160** (c) Jeremy Woodhouse/Getty Images; **161** (c) PhotoLink; **162** (c) PhotoLink.

Illustration

Cover Lynn Chapman; **12** Ken Bowser; **43** Chris Lensch; **46** Ken Bowser; **72** Joe Lemonnier; **74** Bernard Adnet; **77** Sally Vitsky; **104–106** Dan Andreason; **108** Nathan Jarvis; **167** Sally Vitsky; **116–130** Rene King Moreno; **132–135** Robert Schuster; **135** Robin Boyer; **137** Patrick Gnan; **139** Ken Bowser; **142** Nathan Jarvis; **144–162** Richard Bernal; **164–165** Ken Bowser; **164–166** (props) Pamela Thomson; **166–167** Ken Bowser.

All other photos Houghton Mifflin Harcourt Photo Libraries and Photographers.